THE CHIROPRACTIC WEBSITE ESSENTIALS

Everything You Need to Know About Creating A
Winning Website to Help Grow Your Practice

Jon Morrison

©2020 Get Clear Consulting

THIS IS NOT FOR ALL CHIROPRACTORS

In fact, for those who don't have a desire to grow their practice this could be a catalyst for chaos.

This resource isn't for those who wish to take advantage of people's ignorance with pseudo-science that scares them into long-term care plans and is desperately trying to up-sell them with products they don't really need.

This resource is a powerful piece of literature. If you get a hold of the following principles and actually apply them to your website, you will be set up to make the income and impact that you've always wanted.

THIS WAS MADE FOR YOU IF YOU:

Are an Evidence-Based Chiropractor

We love to help people who love to help. If you are committed to delivering patient-centred care that is rooted in the best scientific research, we want to help you reach more people, helping them get better.

Have Excellent Systems in Place

There is little use for providing you with a steady stream of new patients if your systems cannot handle it. You need to have the infrastructure in place to stay organized, fully present with patients, and the management skills so that we are not inviting new patients into chaos.

Are Looking for A Tool to Help More People Get Out of Pain

There is a lot of stress when it comes to marketing your practice. There are thousands of different tools out there that you can use. Having a great website is just the beginning of feeling great about how you spread the word about your practice.

IT'S TIME TO STOP FEELING EMBARRASSED ABOUT YOUR WEBSITE

We've worked with and spoken to thousands of chiropractors about their marketing. Most of them despise their website.

Too many chiropractors confess to feeling ashamed of their website, the first impression people get when being introduced to their practice. When we look at their sites, hoping to console them, we discover that their embarrassment is appropriate. Sadly, there are a lot of lousy websites out there.

The best DCs deserve the best tools to help them reach the most people.

In the following pages, you will learn the four essential components of a winning website.

Let's diagnose the problem before getting into the solution.

Today is a new day.

You don't have to feel

ashamed of your

website anymore.

WHY MOST WEBSITES DON'T WORK

There are four major problems that cause most chiropractic websites to fail. They suffer from one (sometimes all four) of these problems:

1. They Lack Eye-Catching Design

Too many websites are built with generic themes that are cluttered, dated or just don't look right.

As a result, a browser will take a quick look and because it looks ugly, make a judgment about the business (sometimes unfairly) and move on to a competitor's site.

2. The Words Don't Compel People to Action

The problem with just "having a website" is that everyone has a website these days. When businesses do not pay attention to the actual words they have on their website, they often confuse a prospective client, or they simply do not compel them to engage.

3. They Get Buried by Google

Having a website that is beautiful and captures the attention of visitors is incredible to have. Still, if it doesn't speak to Google as well and get recognized for the keywords people are searching for, the business goes invisible online.

4. Making Edits Is Tough and Slow.

Whether you get slowed down by confusing software or held hostage by your developer, most chiropractors get fed up with how difficult it is to make changes that they give up creating content on their site.

Any combination of the above four problems results in a website that does not work was a total waste of time and is costing the business a ton of money in lost sales.

THE SOLUTION: THE FOUR CHIROPRACTIC WEBSITES ESSENTIALS

1. **Beautiful Design** that makes you look professional.

2. A **Clear Message** that captures the attention of your ideal patient.

3. **Strong SEO** that works in partnership with Google, so you get the best ranking.

4. **Easy to Edit** so you can keep your content fresh and up to date.

ESSENTIAL #1 - BEAUTIFUL DESIGN

Have you ever read a book with an ugly cover? Not likely.

Even though we are well into the 21st century and supposed to be more civilized than ever before, we are still pretty shall. Despite what our parents and teachers taught us, we still make judgements about books based on their covers. We do the same for people with their clothes and company's websites.

It's just human nature to make a judgement about someone based on how they present as a first impression. Your website is the front door of your practice. Ten times out of ten, people will visit your website before visiting your office. We can never figure out why no good chiropractor would ever want the front of their office to be messy, ugly, and dated and yet they are willing to put up with that on their website.

The good news is that after this section, you will have some practical, actionable steps to clean up the online front of house on your website.

How to Present Well Online

Here are some of the design principles that you should be incorporating on your website:

1. Choose Three Colors

It's one of those things that you don't learn about in chiropractic school. You need to build a recognizable brand. The best chiropractic brands have only three colors. They have primary, secondary and tertiary colors. These are often expressed as HEX#'s. There are several helpful sites that offer a variety of options for colors that work well together.

Below are some examples from our friends at Design Wizard. Notice how the numbers each contain a HEX code, so you get exact color.

2. Pick Two Complementary Font Pairings

On your website, you want only two fonts: one for the headlines and one for the paragraphs. Your website building software should come with all sorts of fonts you can get for free.

Not sure which ones work well together? Just Google "Best font pairings." You'll get plenty of help. See the example to the right of how you can use two fonts.

3. Break Up Text with Headlines, Sub-headlines And Short Paragraphs

Due to the nature of how people scan content online these days, you need to keep your paragraphs short.

> **THIS IS A HEADLINE TO CATCH ATTENTION**
>
> *This is your sub-headline to draw people in.*
>
> This is the body of the paragraph in a new font. Here is where you provide the actual content of your message.
>
> It's the "good stuff". But to get people to this point, you have to win them with headlines.

The public doesn't read material online like a journal or a textbook. We scan everything. You have to win people's attention with inviting headlines and sub-headlines.

Make sure your content is no more than three lines per paragraph.

4. Include Lots of White Space

Whatever you do, don't clutter up your website by trying to put everything on it. For every word or image included, you need to offset it with space.

In the website world, we call it "padding." It is just white space around the words and images that give the eyes a little break.

Have you ever been to someone's house and there was stuff everywhere?

You didn't know where to sit or stand. It was just stressful. That's what cluttered websites do. Look at a top brand like Apple, for instance. Notice they don't have text and images taking up every square pixel.
It's all perfectly spaced out so that your eyes can focus on just one thing.

This is an extreme example of what not to do.

Don't clutter up your website. Because it is intuitive, people may not thank you personally for it, but they will respond better because of it.

5. Quality, High-Resolution Pictures of Happy, Healthy People

Here's a rule of thumb when it comes to choosing picture for your site: *Use high-quality pictures of healthy, happy people.*

Blurry, dated images will affect your brand more than any of us would like to admit. While those free images we find online are nice because they are free - many of them are cheesy. They are especially bad if they are blurry or pixelated.

While we all know that budgets can be tight enough already, there is nothing like getting quality images from a paid site. You also could get free ones by taking them yourself or some of the free images sites that are easy to find these day.

Can You Tell the Difference?

Cluttered

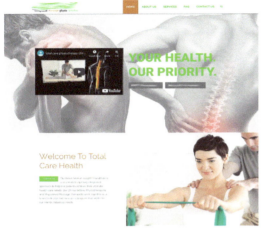

Clean

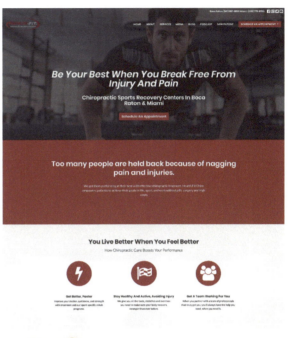

ESSENTIAL #2: A CLEAR MESSAGE

If you find yourself struggling to talk about what you do, don't worry, you're not alone.

You know a lot about your area of expertise but relaying all that information can sometimes confuse and overwhelm your potential clients.

Taking the time to create a clear marketing message is the best way to create words that quickly tell others what you do.

Lee Lefevre wrote in his book *The Art of Explanation* about a condition that you may be suffering from but have never been diagnosed. He calls it "The Curse of Knowledge." It means that when you think and talk at the highest levels of your industry, you likely have a hard time communicating what you do to others. I get why it happens to chiropractors.

All-day long, you are thinking at a level nine or ten (out of ten) trying to help your patients.

You have your education, CE courses, stuff you read on the Internet from peers - you've got nicknames and acronyms for everything. Now you need to translate it to the public. They've never heard any of these abbreviations or multi-syllable words.

Now you've got to tell them about how you can help them. Doctors who suffer from the curse of knowledge talk way over their current and potential patient's heads. They miss an opportunity to make a critical connection.

Now imagine trying to find the right words to talk about themselves and their practice clearly and make it engaging and interesting for prospective patients.

It's a missed opportunity waiting to happen.

The good news is that with a little work, you can have a clear message that you use to speak and write at a level your ideal patient will easily understand.

The Benefits of a Clear Message:

Taking the time to get into the head and heart of your ideal patient helps you stand out in a noisy world.

Speaking clearly has many benefits. A clear message:

- Helps you identify your ideal patient and understand what they desire most.
- Enables you to engage those you aim to serve while keeping essential details about your product and services simple and easy to remember.
- Identifies the struggles they are facing in a way that the words capture their attention (people get hooked when you talk about their problems)
- Strategizes a plan for establishing your company as the best solution for patients to come to you for solutions to their problems.
- Establishes what success looks like for your clients and then focuses our efforts on marketing towards that.

We've helped chiropractors all over North America get over the curse of knowledge. The first step is to create what we call a *Brand Messaging Guide*.

You'll get an overview on it on the following page.

Most chiropractors have trouble talking about what they do. Taking the time to create a clear message helps immensely.

HOW TO CREATE A BRAND MESSAGING GUIDE

Work through the list of questions below before you try to put any words on your website.

You should take the time to answer these to make sure you have clarity around who you are speaking:

1. What does our ideal patient want in life (as it relates to chiropractic)?
2. What is the problem that is stopping them from getting it?
3. What is it doing to them?
4. Why should they trust us to provide the solution?
5. What is the first step ("Call to Action") that we want them to take?
6. What is our process for helping them?
7. How can we describe the ideal outcome for them?

Now You Can Create A One-Liner and Elevator Pitch Which Are Helpful for The Copy on Your Home Page.

Here Are Some One-Liners Our Clients Have Used for Their Practice:

- Feel better and get back to doing the things you love.
- We take care of your pain so you can take care of your family.
- We have whole devoted to helping you feel great again.
- Enjoy your life, free from pain.
- Don't wait to live an independent, pain-free life
- Rediscover the thrill of doing what you love.
- Be your best when you break free from injury and pain.

Here's How You Do Your Own Pitch:

1. Start with one of the above problems.
2. Tell us you know what it's like to encounter it.
3. Show us the solution.
4. Tell us what we should do about it.

Here Are Some Examples to Inspire You:

- "Too many people are unsatisfied by the level of care after an injury. At _____ we have a client-centred model that takes time to listen to the goals of each patient and gives them the treatment and plan to help them achieve those goals."

- "Dealing with an injury can be devastating to your work and family life. At _____ (your practice), our team provides the personal care you need so that you can get back to feeling great at work and at home."

- "A growing number of people in Vancouver are frustrated because of their nagging injuries are keeping them from everyday activities. We have a treatment plan that helps them break free from the pain so that they can get back to enjoying all that life offers them."

- "Too many people are full of anxiety because it seems like surgery is the only solution to their pain. At _____ , we offer chiropractic treatment based on the best scientific evidence that keeps you off the surgeon's table so that you can enjoy your life - pain-free."

When you have the answers to these questions, you have a foundation upon which to build out your website.

HOW TO APPLY YOUR BRAND MESSAGE TO YOUR WEBSITE

Having worked on hundreds of chiropractic websites, this is the layout we have found has the most success.

- Banner image or video of your ideal patient enjoying a healthy, happy life at the top of your home page.
- Headline cast a vision for the best outcome your patient wants to achieve.
- Sub headline that describes what you do.
- Clear button with your call to action below the headline.
- State the problem that your potential patients are struggling with? We believe the best place to put this is "below the fold"
- Use icons, images or badges to show the benefits your patients can expect.
- Section and picture that introduces you as the one who will lead them out of their problems and into a better life.
- Badges or logos of certifications which show your credibility (without confusing people).
- Testimonials that show how you have solved problems a potential patient may be facing today.
- Value stack of the services you offer.
- Do you have a place at the bottom for all the random information someone might need quickly (phone, email, location, and anything that doesn't fit)?

Other "Must-Haves" For Your Pages:

About Page:

- Make empathetic statements showing that you have compassion for someone suffering from pain. ("We/I understand how frustrating it is…" or "We know how hopeless it can feel about going from treatment to treatment and nothing works…")
- Talk about what makes you an authority. List where you went to school, some CE credentials or niche certifications you have collected along the way.
- List some hobbies and interests to make a personal connection.
- Briefly mention your family.
- Include a picture of you and your team to make it more personal.

Service Pages:

- Write a headline that a newspaper might use if they were featuring the service. Include the keywords you would like to be found on a Google search.
- Describe your services in simple language, making sure you include information that is helpful to the patient (not just what you like to talk about).
- Talk about the benefits of those services to the patient.
- Give a quick overview of how you complete the service.
- Bring it to life with images of the service in action or some happy outcome they can achieve because of the service.
- Include a call to action.
- Add a contact form at the bottom in case they have more questions.

Contact Page:

- Your name, address, phone number, and email exactly matching your Google My Business page.
- A map that is integrated with Google Maps.
- Contact form so an inquirer can reach you directly.

ESSENTIAL #3 - STRONG SEO

We all want to be on the first page of a Google search.

That is precious real estate and getting there can mean a huge boost in new patients. The problem is that not everyone gets there and the ones who do have to work hard at it.

It's Not Easy Playing the SEO Game - But It Is Simple

Think about the last Google search you did. There were only 15 spots available on that coveted first page.

You have 2-3 ads to start. That cost someone money to be there. Then a map comes up as you scroll. That also has a paid position at the top. That spot costs money too. Then there are three more map listings for those who are blessed and highly favoured by the Google gods. Then you have 6-8 organic listings.

Those are the ones with whom most of us would be most happy. The problem is that 3 of them are enormous domains like Yelp, or MyBestRated, or RateMyMd or other Goliaths that like that which are hard to defeat. The truth is that even the people who run those four spots are SEO experts charging $500-700 a month to get their clients there.

Is it worth it to even try to play Google's game?

It is always worth it to play Google's game. While I must confess that I have been in and out when it comes to playing the SEO game, I always end up seeing the value in it.

Why? Because I have compassion for the person who is doing the Google search. That's someone's dearly loved daughter, son, friend, co-worker. They have a real problem that has disrupted their dream. They are searching for answers. They are looking for someone to help. They do not know some of the traps that are awaiting them masquerading as "chiropractor."

I don't want innocent people getting caught up in some doctors forever treatment plan that never works because it is based on pseudo-science. Each day I strive to help the best people leverage the best tools to reach more people. Because of this, we must outrank competitors.

How To Improve Your Partnership with Google:

1. Create Excellent Content

Content is always king with Google. It's been that way for over a decade. People are looking for answers to questions and Google is trying to find the best possible resource for them.

The algorithm has changed many times over the years, but this principle never changes: *Content is king.*

When you partner with Google to help people, your website becomes that resource.

To be a resource, you need to provide value for your visitors. Being a resource means you must be valuable to other people who are searching. You need to know what they are searching for so you can meet the need.

It is critical to figure out the keywords for which you want to rank. Works like "chiropractor in (your city/town), back pain, massage therapy, sports injury, and all the variations of those words are the searches for which you want to show up.

Write for People, Not Algorithms

This is important to remember: You are not writing for Google. You are writing for people. Don't just repeat variations of your keywords throughout a page. Keyword jamming is a dated SEO strategy and these days it could do more harm than good. You'll certainly be penalized, especially when your content doesn't make any sense and people stop reading.

What YOU Should Write About

Keep your content fresh and relevant to what you know your patients will want to read. You're doing the writing, correct? Does a freelance copywriter from Fiverr or Upwork know your patients? Not likely. They could learn, but no one knows better how to talk with them like you and your staff.

Blogs That You Should Write That Give Your SEO A Boost:

- o How do I choose the best chiropractor in (your city) for my family and me?
- o What are the benefits of having a family chiropractor?
- o What is chiropractic care?
- o 5 questions you should ask your chiropractor in (your city)?
- o How do I choose a chiropractor in (your city)?

I'm amazed by how many people are wasting time and money, thinking that they can produce content that no one they know will ever read.

Remember that the goal is not to hack Google's algorithm or gain the system in some way. The goal is to partner with Google to provide the content for which people are looking.

To make sure you're doing this, at the end of every piece of content you write, ask:

1. Will this help anyone?
2. Would *I* read this?
3. Would my patients find it interesting?

If the answer is "No" to any of the above, the content you post may actually do more harm than good. There are many stories out there of sites that used to have a great ranking take a nosedive when people clicked on a page, but then bounced once they realized the page was not helpful at all.

2. Include Videos

Video is powerful. It keeps people engaged. When they are engaged, they stay on your site longer. When they are on your site longer, Google takes note that you have a helpful site and then improves your ranking for the next person to find you.

Did you know that when it comes to making videos:
- One third of online activity is spent watching them
- 85% of the US internet audience watches videos regularly
- 45% of people watch more than an hour of online videos a week
- Websites with videos have better SEO than ones without[1]

You can do a lot with limited time and budget. Take out your phone (which has a better camera on it than most Hollywood films made in the late 90s), buy about $65 in gear (tripod, light, and lapel mic) from Amazon and talk about what you just told your last patient. It was likely great advice for us all. Your last patient was not the only one struggling with what you told him.

What Kind of Videos Should You Make?

Stretches and Exercises

Set up a tripod with a wireless microphone (attach it to your phone and use the voice memo app for a nice hack) and talk through some helpful stretches and exercises.

You can use these videos to show patients as part of their rehab. They also work well for building your authority and trust.

---

[1] Courtesy of Wordstream Blog. See https://www.wordstream.com/blog/ws/2017/03/08/video-marketing-statistics.

Product Reviews

Highlight a product you like to use or that patients are asking about. Shoot a 3-minute explanation of what you always tell them. It won't be tough to think of what to say. You're already the expert.

Health Tips

What kind of health tips, recommendations, or ideas do you offer your patients repeatedly? Others can benefit from this help as well. Put it on video because you know that's the thing people will pay attention to.

Patient Testimonials

Bring your most successful (and thankful) patients back to the office and have them answer three questions on camera. Not many people will be willing to do a monologue but not many resist an interview with you there beside them (you can stay off-camera).

Ask these three questions:

1. What was it like struggling with your condition before you came in?
2. What was it like getting treatment here?
3. What has it been like since you got better?

A Commercial About Your Practice

This is your "commercial" video for your practice. Talk about your passion to help patients, techniques you use, give a tour of the building or whatever you want to do to show off the practice.

Just be warned: While we video creators' default to this type of video, it is also the least interesting to others.

My Advice for Making Engaging Videos

I'll always remember this bit of advice (it doesn't come naturally to me either, but it's critical if you want to make an engaging video):

Think of the natural amount of energy you'd give in a conversation and then double it on video.

And then double it again.

And remember that if you can't hit pause and catch yourself making an awful face, you're still not putting enough energy into it.

Even marketing guru, Gary Vaynerchuk, confesses he looked like he was in a hostage situation in his early videos.

Just start. You'll get better as you go.

3. Do Some Local SEO

Every chiropractor can grow their business and attract more patients using local SEO strategies. According to Google, 46% of searches have a 'local intent'. That means, people are searching not for some universal principle or "best cookie recipe", they are looking for an expert "near me."

This section highlights some of the most important principles about getting found by the people searching near you.

Create and Optimize Your Google My Business Listing

When it comes to ranking well on Google, there has been a clear move by the search engine giant to favor those who have optimized their Google My Business listing (that's what Google calls your business listing that shows up when people search for you).

If you have not set up and optimized your listing, you are missing out on a huge opportunity.

Your listing must include information such as:
- Correct website, address, phone number, and hours as it is given on your site (make sure they are EXACTLY the same)
- Plenty of photos
- Service categories (chiropractic, massage, physical therapy, etc.).

See the example on the right of an excellent Google My Business listing.

4. Get Lots of Reviews

Your reputation matters.

You know that before making a purchase online you are going to do some digging around to see if it is a worthwhile product. While it's

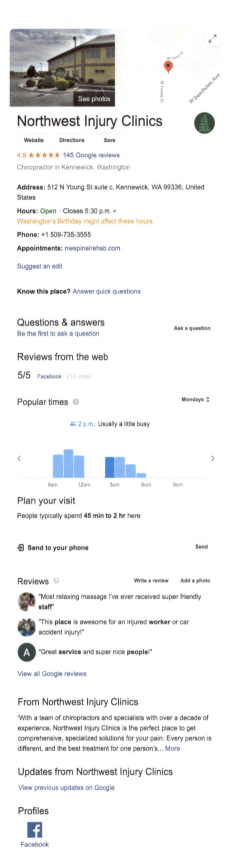

interesting to find out what companies are saying about themselves, what really interests you is what customers are saying about the product.

It's the same as finding a chiropractor. Your marketing message is important BUT having an outstanding reputation as a doctor who gets results for their patients while treating them well in the process - that's the gold standard.

Find a system that delivers you a steady stream of outstanding Google Reviews. There's helpful software out there that can follow up with patients and link to your Google account. But if you're not interested in paying another subscription, there's always the cost-effective way of printing off a piece of paper to put beside your reception desk. And of course, if you hear a patient raving about their experience just memorize this line:

"That's so encouraging. I'm glad to hear about it. Do you know what is so helpful to both our staff and others? If you go online and leave a Google Review. We know there are a lot of people reading those, and your story could benefit a lot of people."

Why Are Reviews So Important?

1. The effect of your Google ranking. If someone searches "Best Chiropractor near me", Google has it in the algorithm to do everything **not** to promote a practice that consistently gets lousy reviews.

2. It encourages engagement. They can affect the number of people click through to your website. Great reviews generate interest! Poor reviews encourage them to keep scrolling by.

3. It sways people to book with you. With many fantastic reviews, people will be more comfortable to book themselves into your care.

5. Own the Keywords

If you haven't already, make a list of words that you would like to show up for when someone is searching.

Let's use the example of how to rank well when someone is searching for "Chiropractor/Massage/Physical Therapy in _____ (Your City)."

Put variations of the words "Chiropractor" and "Your City" in:

- The title tag of the site
- The heading or subheading of your home page
- The URL (www.yourdomain.com/yourcity)
- Your content
- Alt tags
- The site's meta description

Warning: Don't overuse the exact phrase: "Chiropractor In _____ (City)" repeatedly. You will be punished for keyword jamming. Use variations and get creative.

Optimize Your Contact Page

Make sure the information on your contact page matches the information on your Google My Business Listing. Google doesn't want to look bad so make sure that when they tell someone your phone number and address, that's the real number and address!

Finally, it is best practice to include an embedded Google Map on your contact page or in your footer. Don't think too much about why this is so, just do it.

6. Make Sure Your Website Itself Is SEO Friendly

Your website is a major factor for how well you do on your Google ranking. The best sites include the following characteristics:

Fast-Loading

Have you ever Googled something, clicked on one of the listings and then hit "Back" because you stared at a blank screen for three seconds? That slow page load resulted in lost business for the company. The quick "bounce" hurt its Google ranking as well. Google will not be as quick to send people there in the future.

You want to make sure your site loads quickly. You can keep a nice trim site by using smaller images, fewer plugins, and minimal JavaScript. If you don't know what those mean, your web developer will, and they can help.

If you're not sure if your site is fast there are several free site speed tests that can be found with a simple search. Google offers one, including recommendations to improve your speed.

Site Security

Web encryption has been around for years, but it wasn't until 2018 that it became obvious which sites were secured and which ones weren't. While an explanation exceeds the scope of this book, the difference between an unsecured site (HTTP://www...) and a secure site (HTTPS://www...) makes a difference in how your site scores.

Google announced in 2015 that it would favor sites that use HTTPS over those that don't. While site security is most critical for e-commerce and has little benefit for a chiropractic site, no member of the public wants to be warned that a chiropractor's site is "Not Secure" when they are browsing.

Mobile-Friendly

Every year people spend more and more time on their mobile devices and tablets. The problem is that many websites still aren't designed to account for different screen sizes and load times. A mobile-friendly site changes its layout from desktop to tablet and phone.

The design moves to a vertical configuration, bringing on a different display of content and pictures.

When Can You Expect to See Results?

"How long until I can expect to see results?" is the great SEO question of our time.

The truth is that the timeframe is entirely out of our control. As my SEO expert friend says, "Sometimes you just have to throw your hands in the air and confess that you are entirely at the mercy of Google."

Google seldom skyrockets newcomers to the top. It wouldn't be fair if they did. Someone could set up a fake business with an SEO-perfect website today and dominate the market instantly, causing all kinds of fraud charges, upset users, and a disrupted industry.

This would be a disaster for Google as it would make headline news and cause people to lose trust in Google.

It is reasonable to expect results in 4-6 months, depending on:

1. **How your site is doing already.** Are you ranking well or are you being penalized for some shady link-building campaign that has your site grouped with gambling and porn sites in Eastern Russia?

2. **What is your competition doing?** You are not competing for page one with every chiropractor in North America or even in your state. You're just up against the other local doctors around you. Are they doing well with SEO? If they are, they will be tougher to outrank. If there's not a lot of competition, you'll see better results.

3. **Your execution.** How well you apply the principles recommended in this booklet will affect how you rank. If people start responding to the changes you make, you will be rewarded accordingly.

You've Got This

It's great to be SEO-friendly but don't be obsessed about it. The points covered in this section are some little things you can do that will help boost your ranking.

You don't have to be an SEO Guru. You don't have to hire some ridiculously expensive agency.

Just partner with Google to provide the best possible experience for those looking for answers. At the end of the day, it's all about helping people. As an Evidence-Based Chiropractor, you know all about that. So just go do your SEO and be yourself.

ESSENTIAL #4 - EASY TO EDIT

In the old days, when you wanted to have a winning website because sites were so complex to build, you had to hire an outside agency to make it for you.

While that is fine, it's tough when they create the site and then never give you the keys to it.

Several problems quickly emerge.

I call it "The Lousy Site Cycle".

Here's the Lousy Site Cycle Played Out:

1. The site slowly goes out of date as staff members move on, and new ones come in.
2. It is tough to add new material because you have to email your content to the company that is managing your site for you.
3. You noticed replies to your emails taking longer and longer.
4. You noticed spelling or grammatical mistakes, but it's too frustrating of a process to bother requesting a change.
5. The content gets stale.
6. The overall site starts to look dated.
7. You get embarrassed and discouraged about your website.
8. You stop talking about your website.
9. Your website does nothing to help you grow your practice and you live each day with the burden that you need a new website.

10. You resign that websites are a waste of time and money because they don't do anything to help.

Sound familiar? This is why most chiropractors despise their website, or even the prospect of thinking or talking about it.

This situation created a market for easy-to-use website builders that empowered regular people to be able to build their own websites. With these platforms we now have affordable, pre-built templates that look great as soon as you buy them, coupled with drag-and-drop software that allows you to create a page with no coding.

The power is now yours to have a website that is not held hostage by a web design company, it stays where it should be with you.

The Benefits of Being Able to Make Changes Yourself:

1. SEO boost.

Remember that for SEO, content is king. If you don't have fresh content going up online, your site will become stale.

2. You'll do more of it.

If adding content is fun, simple, and quick, you'll love doing it and be encouraged to do more. If updating your site is slow, cumbersome and confusing, you're not going to do it as it'll feel like a chore.

3. You won't have outdated information on your site.

If you keep your website up to date, people will stop asking for that massage therapist that hasn't been around for two years (but they're still advertised on the site like they are). Outdated information makes you look bad. It needs to be fresh and accurate.

4. You can train your administrators to update the site.

Imagine if you were not the one who had to update the hours, the staff pages, images, or the content. If you have a simple editor, you can train your staff to login, make edits, create new content, and take responsibility for the site.

Feel Like You Own It

Having served the chiropractic community for several years, I know how important this point is: You must feel like you own your own site. I don't mean the proprietary rights to the coding - I mean the site content itself.

If you feel like your website is something separate from your practice, I guarantee you are not leveraging the potential of this digital front door to your practice.

I know that most people with no experience do not feel comfortable building a site from scratch (and the ones that do...it doesn't usually work out so well). While you don't have to create the site from scratch, it is critical that you talk to your web developer about the process of making changes, edits, or upgrades to the site.

COMBINING ALL FOUR ESSENTIALS

Get Clear Sites creates websites that combine everything we talked about above. They look great, speak clearly, rank well on Google, and you'll love growing with it because the easy-to-use platform grows with you.

Here's What Goes into A Get Clear Site:

1. Beautiful Design

Our sites look great on desktops and mobile. We combine compelling images, colours, fonts and a proven structure that help our clients stand out. You don't have to have a degree in design to have an outstanding look to your pages.

2. Clear Messaging

Words are critical on a website. While design attracts, the words compel to action. The framework we use to get into the head and heart of your ideal patients will help you get the words on your site. Each section should tell the story of how you help people solve problems and win their story.

3. Search Engine Optimization Friendly

We know how to talk to people, but we've also learned to talk to Google. We use the best SEO tools and research to find out what people are searching in your area so that Google puts you on top of the ranking. Our clients love watching their site climb higher and higher in Google's ranking.

4. They Are Easy to Use

To feel ownership of a site, you should feel like you can make whatever changes you want. For too long, people have known that they _should be_ able to make simple changes to a website but never had the opportunity. Now they do. Our platform was designed with the end user in mind – and for us, that's anyone ranging from a tech-savvy CEO or someone brand new to the team.

We have designed the website builder that you've always wanted.
Take a look at our website, *getclearsites.com*.

Whatever You Decide to Go with For Your Website, Apply These Principles!

They work.

I assure you that if you take the four essentials of a winning website, you just learned and apply them, your website will work wonders!

YOU SHOULD LOVE YOUR WEBSITE AND WHAT IT DOES FOR YOU

Here's what some doctors recently posted on social media about their experience with their website. We thought it might give you hope.

"We just had a new patient call in and specifically say that the reason she chose us was that she was extremely impressed with our website.
I finally have a website that I like. The site is much more personalized to my style and doesn't spew nonsense like my old stock chiro site. If you're thinking of making a change in your site, I cannot recommend Get Clear Sites enough."

Dr. Joshua Gregory
Hometown Health (hometownhealthoxford.com)

"Jon Morrison and his crew at Get Clear Consulting have been absolutely awesome to work with.
The website is different than the same old thing you always see with chiro websites. They make the message all about the patient (which is what we should be shooting for). I can make changes quickly and the support is there when I need it."

Dr. Aaron Montgomery
Active Motion Spine (activemotionspine.com)

"For years our generic chiro website underperformed for us. Get Clear helped us apply the StoryBrand principles to our site and it immediately started to get us new patients. We are now at the top of a Google search and getting new leads every week."

Dr. Russ Baron
Sun Chiropractic (sunchiro.ca)

"We love our new website.
As fairly new graduates opening our first practice, we have learned there is both a good bit of excitement and nervousness with every decision and purchase you make. From the first phone call we had with Jon, it was obvious we had chosen the right team to work with."

Drs. Zach and Brynn Wurth
Wurth Chiropractic (wurthchiro.com)

"I cannot say enough how pleased I am to have worked with the Get Clear team.

My website turned out wonderfully and the coaching session was very informative as well! I will be recommending Jon and his team to my friends and colleagues."

Dr. Daniel Edwards
Dynamic Health & Performance
(darkecountychiropractor.com)

ABOUT JON MORRISON

We understand that marketing often feels like just another thing you need to do.

You'd probably rather help patients than figure out how to use all the marketing tools out there. It's no surprise that those who are best at caring for people's health struggle to find the margin to market their practice.

Jon Morrison started a group of companies under the "Get Clear" name with a mandate to equip people just like you - the people who are working hard to help others.

We love working with Evidence-Based chiropractors as the focus of our efforts.

Ours is an exciting partnership that has been growing for years. We have been serving our clients, located all over North America, providing them with the help, support, and tools they need to achieve their goals.

This resource came as a result of our success with clients, participation in social media groups, speaking at events, and in constant dialogue with leaders in the profession.

It is our hope that the fruit of all this is that you can enjoy the benefits of a winning website.

You can learn more by visiting our site at getclearsites.com.